Science Around You
Shadows in the Bedroom

Susan Martineau
illustrated by Leighton Noyes

with thanks to Kathryn Higgins,
Head of Chemistry, Leighton Park School

contents

How to be a Scientist

Scientists learn about the world around us by doing experiments.
You will learn about the science in your bedroom in this book.
You won't need any special equipment for these experiments.
They use everyday things you'll probably find at home already.
Don't forget to ask a grown-up before using them.
Before you begin, always read through the whole experiment
to make sure you have everything you need.

BE SAFE!

Never play with the electric sockets and plugs in your bedroom.

Keep a notebook handy so you can draw or write up what happens like a real scientist. You can make up your own experiments too.

Words to Know
Special science words are explained on page 24.

Tidy up your bedroom after you've finished!

Quick Quizzer
answers are on p.24.

Shadow Fun

This experiment is best done at night when it's really dark. Close the curtains and get ready to make some scary shapes. You can make up your own scary or funny ones too.

1. Cut a scary shape out of card.

2. Hold it in front of you, with a plain wall behind it.

3. Shine a torch or lamp on the card.

Quick Fact

In Indonesia they use shadow puppets to put on fantastic shows.

Let's Take a Closer Look!

The holes in the card let the light of the torch or lamp through but the card itself blocks the light. You get a SHADOW on the wall in the shape of the card. A SHADOW is made because the light cannot get through the card.

Try This!

Try putting your hands together as shown to make a horse's head shadow appear on the wall! Put your hands between the lamp and the wall.

See what happens when you move the shape nearer and further from the lamp.

Shine a Light

You need a torch, a piece of foil, a pencil and a dark bedroom for this experiment. Torches are very handy for reading science books (or comics) under the bedclothes!

1. Cover the end of the torch with the foil.

2. Poke a hole in the foil with the pencil.

3. Turn on the torch and shine the light at the things in your room.

Let's Take a Closer Look!

The hole in the foil lets a thin beam of light through. The light travels in a straight line called a LIGHT RAY. Because it is going in a straight line this makes it easy to aim the light at the objects in your room.

Quick Quizzer

What did people use for lights before the invention of lamps?

Light rays are the fastest things in the whole universe.

Try This!

Draw or write down all the things you can think of that make light. Look around your room, the rest of the house or when you are out and about.

clever Eyes

Light bounces off everything we look at and into our eyes. This is how we see things. But our eyes need to let in just the right amount of light. Ask a friend to help with this experiment.

1. Close the curtains.

2. Carefully point a torch upwards so some light shines near one side of your friend's face.

3. Look at each eye and see what is different about the black hole at the front.

Cats can't see any better than us in the daylight!

Let's Take a Closer Look!

The eye in the light has a smaller black hole, or PUPIL, than the eye in the shadows. The PUPIL gets smaller to stop too much light hurting the inside of the eye. The PUPIL gets bigger to let in more light when we need to see in the dark.

Quick Fact

The coloured bit of your eye is called the IRIS. It is the muscle that controls the size of the PUPIL.

Did You Know?

Cats hunt at night and the PUPILS of their eyes can open extra wide to let in as much light as possible for them to see in the dark.

Mirror Magic

Have you ever wondered why you can see yourself in a mirror? Did you know you can use mirrors to look behind you too? You need a friend to help with this mirror magic.

1. Hold a mirror in front of you.

2. Ask your friend to stand behind you.

3. Move the mirror until you see your friend in it!

Let's Take a Closer Look!

You can see yourself in a mirror because LIGHT RAYS bounce off you and into the mirror. The mirror is very shiny and bounces the RAYS back so you see a REFLECTION of yourself. LIGHT RAYS bounce off your friend, too, and on to the mirror. You then see the friend's REFLECTION.

Quick Quizzer!

What do car drivers use to see behind them?

Quick Warning!

Be careful when you are holding mirrors. They can break very easily.

Try This!

See what happens to reflections when you tape two small mirrors together. Put a small object in front of them. Move the mirrors closer and further apart. Count the reflections.

Hold one mirror in front of you and one behind to see the back of your head!

Mad Mirrors

When you look in a mirror you do not always see the reflection you expect to see. This is very useful for tricks! Use a bit of sticky tack to keep the mirror steady.

1. Stand a small mirror upright.

2. Ask a friend to write their name on a piece of paper.

3. Put the paper in front of the mirror.

Let's Take a Closer Look!

Your friend's name looks back-to-front in the mirror! REFLECTIONS are always the wrong way round like this.

If you wave at yourself in a mirror with your right hand, it will look as if you are waving your left. It is called a MIRROR IMAGE.

Try This!

Find a full-length mirror on a wardrobe or wall. Stand very close to the edge of it. Lift one arm and one leg.

If you haven't got a full-length mirror at home, try this in a clothes' shop!

Electric Tricks

We use lots of electricity in our homes to work everything from lights to computers. This kind of electricity moves along wires inside our houses. But there's also another sort of electricity that we can make ourselves.

1. Tear a tissue into small pieces.

2. Find a plastic comb.

3. Comb your clean, dry hair about 20 times.

4. Hold the comb close to the bits of tissue.

Let's Take a Closer Look!

When you run the comb through your hair over and over again this makes STATIC ELECTRICITY build up in the comb. This STATIC ELECTRICITY pulls the tissue paper towards the comb and makes it jump like magic.

Turn the lights off when you leave your bedroom.

Don't waste electricity!

Quick Warning!
Never play with the electric sockets or wires in your house.

Did You Know?
Static electricity builds up in clouds during a thunderstorm. It gets so powerful that it jumps to other clouds or to the ground in the form of a huge spark, or lightning.

Sticking Together

Gather all sorts of things from around your bedroom - cuddly animals, coins, pencils, buttons (plastic and metal), pencils and sharpener, books, keys. You'll also need a magnet.

1. Spread your collection of things on the floor.

2. Touch each one with the magnet.

3. Note down what happens to each object.

If you haven't got a magnet, try a fridge magnet or ask a friend for one.

Let's Take a Closer Look!

The magnet does not stick to everything. Magnets have a special, invisible power that pulls iron and steel things towards it. So most metal objects stick to the magnet but not the things made of paper, wood or fabric.

Quick Quizzer

Will your magnet pick up a pencil?

Try This!

If you have more than one magnet you can test them to see which is the strongest. Make a pile of paper-clips and see which magnet can pick up the most.

Quick Warning!

Never put magnets near to computers, watches or telephones. They can damage them.

Waves of Sound

Sounds are like invisible waves travelling through the air. They are all around us. For this experiment you need to make a cone shape out of a piece of paper.

1. Secure the cone shape with sticky tape. Trim the wide, open end.

2. Tape the cone around one end of some thin, plastic tubing.

3. Hold the open end over a ticking clock or watch.

4. Put the end of the tube just inside your ear.

Let's Take a Closer Look!

The cone collects the sounds of the clock and sends them down the tube to reach your ear. They sound louder because they are being squeezed down a narrow tube. Sound waves normally spread out but the tube is like a narrow path leading them to your ear.

Quick Quizzer

What's the name of the gadget used by doctors to listen to your heart?

Try This!

Hold the cone over your radio or the speaker of your music player. Put the other end of the tube in your ear. Who needs headphones!

Don't push the tube too hard into your ear!

Pulse Power

Your heart pumps blood all around your body. It works harder when you are running about and slows down again when you are sitting still or lying in bed. In this experiment you will see how fast your blood is pumping round.

1. Hold one hand out with the palm up.

2. Look at where the hand joins the wrist, below the thumb.

3. Place the first two fingers of the other hand here.

4. Press down with the flat of those fingers.

Let's Take a Closer Look!

You should be able to feel a flicking movement under the skin. This is your PULSE. Each time your heart beats it is sending blood round your body to give you energy. Each PULSE movement you feel is a heartbeat.

Quick Fact

You can also find a pulse in your neck, your temple, your elbow and even the back of your knee.

Try This!

Jump up and down or bounce on your bed for two minutes. Time yourself with a bedside clock or your watch. Feel how fast your pulse is going now. Then feel again when you have been lying still in bed for five minutes.

If you are fit and healthy it doesn't take long for your pulse to slow down again!

Measure Yourself!

How tall are you? How heavy are you? How big are your feet? Try keeping a Growing Chart for a year to see how you change. Instead of your shoe size you could write in how long your feet are in centimetres.

1. Draw a chart on a large piece of paper, as shown.

2. Every month ask a friend to measure how tall you are.

3. Weigh yourself and write in your shoe size.

4. Keep the chart on your wall or pinned inside a cupboard door.

MONTH	HEIGHT	WEIGHT	SHOE SIZE

Did You Know?

The tallest person ever recorded is an American, Robert Wadlow. At the age of eight he was tall enough to carry his dad up the stairs! He reached 2.72 metres in height.

When you weigh yourself take off your shoes and coat!

Quick Fact

Humans stop growing between the ages of 16 and 19.

Let's Take a Closer Look!

When you are young your body is growing all the time. Ask your friends to keep a Growing Chart of their WEIGHT, HEIGHT and shoe size too. You will see that some people grow more quickly or more slowly than others.

Words to Know

Height – This is the measurement of how tall or high something is.

Iris – The coloured part of your eye. It is the muscle that makes your pupil bigger or smaller.

Light Ray – Light is always moving and travels straight forward in lines. These are called light rays.

Mirror Image – This is the way your reflection looks in the mirror. It is the wrong way round to the real you!

Pulse – The beat or movement made by the blood being pumped round by your heart.

Pupil – The small, round, black hole in the middle of your eye. It is controlled by the iris to let in the right amount of light.

Reflection – You see a reflection when light rays bounce off you and on to a mirror. The light rays bounce back from the mirror and into your eyes.

Shadow – a shadow is made when light cannot go through something to reach the other side.

Static Electricity – This is a kind of electricity that does not move. It is not like the electricity we use for lights and other gadgets.

Weight – This is the measurement of how heavy something is.

Quizzer Answers

Page 7 - candles

Page 11 - a mirror

Page 17 - no. The pencil is made of wood.

Page 19 - a stethoscope